THE TESTIMONY
OF DOVES

BOOKS BY THE AUTHOR

A Cup of Sky with Donald Culross Peattie (Houghton Mifflin, 1950)
A Passage for Dissent: The Best of Sipapu, 1970–1988
    (McFarland Press, 1989)
Freedom to Lie: A Debate about Democracy with John Swan
    (McFarland Press, 1989)
Amy Rose: A Novel (Regent Press, 1995)
Western Skyline (Regent Press, 1995)
Hydra & Kraken or, the Lore and the Lure of Lake-Monsters and Sea-Serpents
    (Regent Press, 1996)
In the Dome of St. Laurence Meteor (Regent Press, 1999)
King Humble's Grave (Regent Press, 2001)
Sweetwater Ranch (Regent Press, 2002)
The Testimony of Doves (Regent Press, 2005)
Inner Life: The Politics of Daydreaming (Regent Press, 2005)

THE TESTIMONY
OF DOVES

NEW POEMS

Noel Peattie

REGENT PRESS
Oakland, CA

ACKNOWLEDGMENTS

The author acknowledges earlier publication of the following poems:

The first part of *Two alphabet poems* appeared as "G minor, G major" in *etc.,*
publication of the Pacific Center for the Book Arts, v. 10, no.4,
February–March 2003.

"Green wheat" was published in the online anthology, *Poets Against the War*
(Sam Hamill, editor), February 2003.

"Two tropical poems" appeared in *Love and Sadistic Dharma*, the California
anthology of poetry, edited by Bradley Mason Hamlin, v. 1, February 2003.

"For a sickness" and "Sleeping late after staying up past midnight" were published
in *Year 2003*, an anthology (Nevada County Poetry Series, William Gainer,
editor), December 2004.

ISBN: 1-58790-115-3

Library of Congress Control Number: 2005920121

Manufactured in the U.S.A.

REGENT PRESS
6020-A Adeline Street
Oakland, CA 94608
www.regentpress.net

CONTENTS

for C=Chris,

once more

2 JANUARY 2003

Leaf-brown sparrows
hunting
through fallen leaves.

Quiet, now:
which is the leaf,

you lynx-eyed,

and which the dun sparrow?

Since now, this month,
the pomegranate tree
has nothing
glorious to display,

what rain healed the far-buried root?
which bird stole the very last seeds?

2 JULY 2004

wait:

note how the slender
branchlet slowly
reaches for the ground

and how one magpie
harshly shoos
the other one (also seeking
seeds) off

and meanwhile towering clouds
gather in the north-north-west

only to pass: die thundering
in the sierras

and leave our trees
thirsty
as usual

THE WAY TO GET THROUGH LIFE,

is to try! yes, how?
to forget
most of it.

Like, all the years at school,
(but not the lifelong friends,

then, the weekends that were joy;
city adventures);

and rather hope for, much later:
vast witty banquets;
at which you'll be honored
__ poems of a lifetime! —
under glittering chandeliers.

And welcome: all goings to bed:
even those
alone:

except the last,

except the last.

A LOUD OAK WOODLAND IN APRIL

The rattle of a woodpecker hammering;
nesting; singing:
everywhere loving,

and I knowing
few birds by their calls:
yet the whole desperation
of life along Pine Creek,
where just before the one-lane bridge,
it meets Salt Creek,
beneath the mingled trees,

is how I need
the knowledge of
you;
who (as I strive to name all things)
I name: the first of all.

MORE WAYS THAN ONE

The way this
tangly
tree kicks up
its legs in
the air,

crooked, desirous, searching eyeless
for room to breathe,

       waiting,
after all that rain

|||\\\\\\\|||//////|.|.|.| ...

till finally in
April! it fills
with blossoms
so orange,

(the color of dreams
just before waking
in the morning),

is the way we greet
the Sun (come
back, up here, star,
leave winter behind!)
with holy love.

A WORD TO TELLUS
(an ancient Roman deity of the earth)

O divinity,

may I,
who will live
only in my poems, be
changed:

even with them: inscribed
on the surface of some
clear
silver urn;

and so,
lie buried till the
forty-first century;

and when dug up
(cleaned, repaired,
strengthened and
polished, by free!
loving hands),

may we not go to
some wealthy collector's
hoard,

but be filled with

tulips of a garden:
not now planted;
and with citrus
of a summer, to be

long hence:
warmed into
calm and happy life.

NOT CONFESSIONAL

Forget about me:
only watch the young tree:

planted, braving its leafage
through a cold spring

wind

COMPLETE HISTORY OF EVERYTHING

In the morning,
soon as sun's up,

waking, joy,
struggle.

Admit defeat? no,
start all over;

bland the afternoon
of limited success.

Did we forget
what we must do always?

compassionate study,
the history
of a lost ant.

Later;
glorious the midnights
of known constellations;
mysteries within.

What is it
starts
with an explosion?

it ends with a stone.

EARLY FEBRUARY

The fly on the cutting-board,
near the coast of the sink,
seeks after crumbs:
her only truth.

Spring! early! sun
at last!
and the desert palm
lifts up its hands
in golden praise.

JUST A NOTE

about the
cold wind
bringing down
all that

stove heat. It's
only mid-
February, but the white

narcissus is
braving up
through lawn dirt,

greeting all of us,
above ground

with fragrant white and
gold beauty,

as every year,
just about this time.

NO TOWER, NO KNIGHT, NO DRAGON

1

The wind, that is the matter of legend,
plays with the trailing branches
of the orchard tree:
tangles of a wild girl
who knows not how to pray

2

gold in abundance
on the plowman's field
this early in the morning

SPRING MORNING

A cloudy sunrise in April,
the pale gold light
on winter wheat,

silence,
blood running in the veins,

warmth of blankets,
no birds calling.

On the other side
of the world:
anger, trouble;

still the leaves of our olive tree
hang unstirred
by the least
wind.

SLEEPING LATE AFTER STAYING UP PAST MIDNIGHT

Freed from dreams
I am delivered to the tender
care of summer bird calls:

finches chattering,
distant quail,
the harsh magpie;
the prophecy
of the solitary dove.

Without the testimony of doves
beyond his windows,
how would a man
keep faith with himself?

THE FIRST DAWN OF SUMMER

The call of the dove,
somewhere in the orchard trees —
the memory of sweet loves:
one far off, now,

others only seen among the silent groves
of bright seasons

long since
slipped away.

THE SPRAY PLANE

at five-thirty in the morning
is the same one
as yesterday at this time:
roaring, forbidding sleep.

It sprays for the tomato hornworm,
a green monster,
burrowing into soft flesh:
the larva of a great dark moth.

I'd rather have the moth;
the pattern of its wings
as it troubles the window screen
offers a message. Can we
read it, guess at it?

It's about what else
is coming to the window:
kind, but inevitable,
night.

THIS PAINTING IS OF:

Arizona:
in the dry wash
tumbleweeds, still green,
and beyond, some thin trees;
to the right, a palo verde.

What survives,
by summer thunderstorms,
flash floods,
roots deep. Beyond the
last green, a notch, blue
against the skyline. It
belongs here,

the way we do not, only
passing through on the
route to the sky.

SENTINEL

In this morning heat
the dove abridges her call:
a short "yáwoo".

Then after the silence,
from some tree,
a brief shriek
I never heard before.

What does the dove hear,
coming down the light
summer wind?

RIGHT ACTION

As your car climbs up the mountain grade,
clears the oak woodland,
you open the window, sudden! the scent of pine,
and so feel lighter, easier,
braver, as the wind makes
sea-music in the branches,

the breath of the pine-wind
is like Right Action
down in the valley below.
There is no equal to Right
Action; as there is nothing
like the Steller's jay,
dressed in blue and indigo;

for these are Right Action:
love at the hearts
of families,
trust among friends, justice
carved in marble,
are like the sparkle of
sunlight among the pine
needles, light
never made by hands.

But when trust is broken: love goes
awry, white pillars collapse
under great pressure, when Right Action
thus is lost,

it is as when the pines are
cruelly felled,
and the jay flies away,
crying fear and anger,
to a wholly separate

part of the wood that is World.

HOT SPELL

amber light at dawn
fan still cooling the room
after the short night

soon the day grows ordinary
sun in milky haze
world to work, I to lie here a moment
and read just one more poem

LETTER TO C:

There's this flock of quail (maybe two flocks),
as I walk near
first one bird, then all together,

they all scatter
aloud, & aloud, &

aloud! they
rise, fly, beyond the
dry weeds, & the
deep inaccessible canyon:

Pine Creek, farther down
it joins Salt Creek. Safe,
the quail are free
of all but soaring red-tail hawks.

Old valley oaks,
lion-skin-dry-grass hills,
jack-rabbits, star-thistles, hi-skying
cirrus, are filled
with summer morning.

Then a pickup
comes out of the ranch
at the end of the road,
and the gate is opened,
parted, closed:
the rancher is off to town.

All of this is holy,
beautiful. Lovely,

I wish you were here.

FOR A SICKNESS

The color of this computer is green,
the child's fever
is red.

O keep her cool.
Cool as green
things, all-a-
growing.

Cool, as the reviving fig tree,
once given up:
springing fresh again,
many-branched:

in a light-wind summer.

LATE AUGUST

After the storm's bluster,
rattle of hail in the road,

clear in the morning:
the knock of neighbor's
hammer on wood;

repairs: on a fence post?
an outside stair?

because the cattle are restless, lowing;
and the old moon needs renewal.

COTTONWOOD POEM

The cottonwood,
all silver, green and
(now)
gold,

trembles in the light fall
wind, —
shivers,

stands still;
and then
is

itself.

DRINKING WHITE WINE

I am at a Hollywood party
friends have taken me to. I am standing
well back from the swimming pool,
under the avocado tree. I notice a planet
coming out in the evening sky. A starlet,
fairly bursting out of her peasant blouse,
comes up to me, we introduce
ourselves, she her new name.
"What do you do?" "I'm a poet."
"Do you write screenplays?" "I never have."
"You should talk to Mr. Molnar, over there.
He'll give you a job writing screenplays."
Someone comes up to her. "Gisela!"
I look at Mr. Molnar, fat hands explaining
success to a small crowd. You have no
business on an African beach,
looking for wave-washed rough diamonds.
They have patrol dogs. Everyone else is
drinking martinis, or Scotch. I am the only one
drinking white wine.

POEM FOR C.

South wind, clouds;
a guess at rain;

the knowledge of love.

GREAT BIRD

Plated and feathered, crimson, gray and gold,
collared in white,
the pheasant stalks among the fallen palm fronds,
patrols the wire fence among the weeds.
Lifting each foot, a small dinosaur,
he stalks for weed seeds, bugs, whatever earth,
gracious, offers his beak.

He lifts off to fly with a loud effort,
lands soon. Maybe some day
his kind will grow so great,
they'll never fly at all,
but run, run, outstripping horse and rider.
But now he hides in the deep green grain.

I do not let him see me.
Hoping the post-dawn dusk of the bedroom
will be concealment, I stay away from windows;
peer, shy as he; make no noise.

Yet should a dog, a car, a sudden hawk,
disturb his adagio prance,
he will fly up, cruise over the new-mown grass,
his double alarm cry
torn
from his red heart.

LATE AUTUMN

Yellow leaves
on the green
back yard —

they talked all summer;

how quiet
they are

now.

Over them, two deer
stepping tenderly,

it's new here,

they're
looking around.

O THE WHITE WIND

o the white wind o
you west wind
winding around the

world

give me some air, give me a
peace of your visiting

release me
from the travail
of this age

COMING HOME AT NIGHT

The pickup truck, ahead of me,
mounts the hump of Road 31
and meets Road 89.

Its back lights glow scarlet
when it stops;
their reflection keeps me
alert.

The half moon tilts
as it nears the horizon ...
who? ... driving along,

will watch the moon
as it lies down;

eight hours to
roll over, & then ... come up
(without a shifting of

gears), from its

mountain east-west
bed?

ONCE MORE

Once more into
the depths the
pool of possibilities
of sun-brown
pebbles the labyrinth of
pillars of light / dark

where the spirit who
only partly
remembers the music

finds the way
by mostly

losing it

TWELVE PAPHLAGONIAN POSTCARDS

1

River east,
river west.
North: blue-black
sea, scarce fish.

2

Mountains cresting south.
Farther up, grasses grow thinner;
only holly,
bitter acorns
for goats' forage.

3

Small kings
(call them princes),
names soon forgotten,
try to collect taxes.
Few silver coins;
expenditures deferred.

4

Not many
soldiers; after invasions, bandits,
nothing much left

to steal.

5

Down to the sea,
valleys rich with
fruit trees;

6

almond first, to blossom;
then pears, plums,
cherries, apricots;

7

walnuts! rolling
down roofs,
all over October;

8

last,
razorback hogs,
fattening on the fall.

9

Winter's north wind,

come out of Scythia.
Sea fog,
storm wrack.
A village's long lost
last boat.

10

Language?
there, you'd have
trouble.
Barter here,
as elsewhere.

11

Our girls,
dark hair,
olive blushes;

stay pure;
sing wedding songs,
till almost
your best midnight.

12

Our poets,
their epics,

ancients' proverbs,
everyone's daily oaths:

died out,
none written;
all our turns of speech:
well,
lost to your scholars.

MARCH 2004

Four weeks before
the swallows
the first almond blossoms
fly in the earliest

merciful wind. But the pomegranate
is still bone-brown,
and its buds,
closed, russet,
are not easily
visible.

Springing up
rejoicing, is
what they've
yet to do. Is this the secret way
the body suddenly flowered,

those twenty
centuries
ago?

MESSAGE FROM A BOTTLE

The cork,
surmounted by a pewter
ring, then
to a buoy
of the same
metal
harbors the wine,
inside.

Its little sailboat, moored,
is secure, but swelling jib
and mainsail, would
swing it to starboard if
it were afloat. And if
I picked it up by
its silver braided
cable, the mast would go

down, head first
oh oh!

Thin north wind?
that's that
port rack
wind. Late in the season.
Where to, now?

SECRETS

Concerning nipples,
everyone has them;
hiding under shirts,
lifting them, they are
palpably shaped
for the lips of lover or child,
as Q is destined for U.

Do not, as some evildoers do,
torment them, twist them;
but seek them,
fly to them,
touch them lightly, deeply,
make them bloom like roses.

They are sealed doors to the body.
Respect them, adore them.
The left one, most precious,
soonest revealed,
lies just over
the beating heart.

POSTER GODDESS

Naked, she rides through the heavens,
serious, her cycle has
wings on the pedals. No blonde coed
has hair that long, never splitting,
blowing down to her feet.
She is Aphrodite, who else?
goddess of love. On a bicycle!

To be her child, to suck her milk
from the pale nipple; to be her son,
champion, carrying her banner
(white, a capital A made
out of flowers), into the New
World. Valiant, all night long,
until her home, the moon,
withdraws behind her mountain curtain.

The doe belongs to her too,
the one I saw yesterday
prance over the low fence, and disappear
into the deep canyon of Pine Creek. And the
dove is her attribute, the low moan of her.

And even the dead spider in your window screen.

TWO ALPHABET POEMS

The letter G,

invented by Spurius Carvilius Ruga,
and displacing Z,

begins *greed*, and *grip*, and *ghost*.

But if it scares with *goblin*,
it also discloses *girlfriend*.

If it is born in *gloom*,
it also rises in *glory*.

And though it leads through *grave*,
it aims for, approaches, *God*.

(And they brought Z back at the end).

Thank you, father Ruga.

And now ...

****

The letter U,

begins *Uganda*, *Ukraine*,
Uruguay, *United States*,
and other *Uniteds*,

too numerous to mention.

If it begins *uncomfortable*,
as in *uniform*,
even *ugly*,
nay
unendurable,

it begins *uncle*,
urbane, even *useful*, as in
umbrella.

The ancient Archbishop began thus:
Unguo te in regem
I anoint thee king

and I alter
his benediction
thus:

Unguo te in reginam
I anoint thee queen
in tempore belli
in this sad time

cordis mei
dearest C,

of my heart.

AMBER

1

is the
light of
after noon
blessing the house

and the rows of tomatoes
neighbor planted only last
week, and
will they
last before
frost?

2

night-time
is for reading
old poems or
waiting your next message

A DIFFERENCE OF FIFTY-THREE YEARS

Here is a magazine called *Seventeen*.
It comes out on the stands every month.
The girl on each cover is welcome
as cherry pie; she's tubbed, pure,
her hair is up, or ribboned.
Her life is all dresses,
parties, and little pink wishes.
She says to the world, Oh hurry,
hurry up, *please*, and it does.

Here is a man about seventy.
Why isn't there a journal called *Seventy*?
Because he isn't as welcome;
because nobody wants to be like him.
He says to the world, Slow down;
my flat feet can't keep up with you.
He whispers, I'm still alive.

But it doesn't slow down, the world.
It keeps on hurrying; for, see there,
an impatient virgin is waiting.

(Every day, an old man is buried).
Every month, there's another young girl.

NEWS FROM THE GARAGE

Parking the car,
I saw in the dusky space
a vibrant small wasp:

lovely colors:
French ultramarine,
shaken with silver —

tremble as she hunted
among the cobwebs
for a safe place to

build a nest,
find a spider,
sting it near to death,
bring it to her mud home,

and right there, beside it, to
lay and hatch her
terrible colony of eggs.

CALLING

I telephoned my legislator,
said, Hey Mister,
vote YES on Assembly Bill 189.
Did it. Right!
Had lunch.   Now, what was his name?

... a late noon dove,
in slowly
rising heat,
"whoo? whoo"?

The man in the sunflowers: while I'm
driving by on Road 31.
What is he seeking, among that
city of cities,
each a golden spiral
explored by bees?

And what wild bird
is calling, singing us along,
going west?

HERE, HOLD THIS

and don't drop it;
lose it;
it's as you know
all-important;
hot on the bottom, heavy,
it's what helps keep the two
Americas together;
slippery, I know,
where it reaches into mantle,
(the Canal, a trifling skin scratch, is
there, a little off to your left
side). Oops! careful, hold up
your end, it's a range like a bone
near the surface of the planet. There! You've got it
wedged back in,
nearly. Now give it a push,
a kick won't
be enough,
it'll take all
your strength to
get it in the right place. AT
LAST! the continents are joined together,
way they've been,
ever since the Miocene. Whoever
loosened it is
going to be real sorry. Now,
let's wash our hands
in the oceans, you on
your sea, I on

mine. THAT'S
done. Now, we can go indoors for
lunch.

TO A POET TEN THOUSAND YEARS HENCE

we were as moths
sucking the moon

our skills will be crushed
by the latter
ice

but can't you read the messages
on our blood-

drenched pebble-
stones?

I FINISHED READING YOUR POEM

and I said, "excellent good,"
and that last "good" isn't superfluous;
you ended your poem exactly right,

like clapping a red wool tasseled cap
on the head of a small child
who is at last! properly dressed
for a walk on a bright fall day.

INCIDENT

She broke into a
coughing fit, and you
know it, coughing is a
way of life, beginning, then it takes
hold of you. Another friend
made her raise her arms, she
did, and said, My side hurts.
(After a while the problem
begins to be seen as having
always been inevitable). It was
noon time, and meanwhile,
the rest of us, knowing
a business meeting would be
starting soon, got on with our own
desperate lunches.

TWO WINDY DAY POEMS

1

See the torment
of the leaf-shadows
on the window blind
in the north wind

and the hurrying
of the clouds
driven overhead

2

Up flew the little yellow-
winged bird
into the bush
so that I might not identify
her species from a book

nor guess at
her desperation

THE FOAL, TOLD

We were all told
that
up on "Mares' Hill"
where the barn was,

a young mare was
going to have her foal.
Told to keep away?

yes, we all did;

until the young
girls crept up
to look for
the little
foal
standing by the
mother: seeing
through who knows
what slats,
windows, breathing-
holes?

We boys were told to
keep, keep
away.

It was their business,
hers:

and hers, and hers.

No mistaking the maiden voices.
We, held back.

When the foal
appeared, at last,
it was for us, just
one more horse:

too little, too staggery,
to even try,
to ride.

"Looking up through the leaves,"

an empire of green;
at the organ keyboard,
an ocean of music.

Late in life's afternoon,
I've got enough foliage

to invade, to clear away,
this fall;

in sounds,
to drown in.

pease please

pease porridge hot

please pour it cold

please pass the little

moon

two days old

some think it hot

some call it cold

some love

    the

        little

        moon

     two days

old

NEW RAIN

While I'm finishing
lunch,
looking out the window at
the shuddering
tree branches,
I estimate
the approach of the storm:
for the dun light is paler
than the thirsty
earth;

and the new rain, we need it,
is gathering its strength,
and
soon will rush out of
the merciful
ocean.

CIRCLING

The moth,
an inch below the ceiling,
circles round and round,
while the bedside lamp
gives her a shadow;
closely follows her.

Is she a soul seeking rest,
a question wanting an answer?

She hopes to find a tiny bit of water,
in the cat's dish,
drink quietly,

and, please,
not tip over and
drown,

as did the wasp
I found this morning
dead in the kitchen sink.

She is so much more than her

shadow.

GREEN WHEAT

The week's wind, tired,
dies down at sunset. (On the Net
crowds mass, voices threaten)

but now comes the last poem
of the day. The winter wheat,
skin of the world,
relieved of the north's ruffling,
stands erect, alert,
every green blade attentive
to the next day's kindly sun.

THE SHOVEL UNDER THE TREE

To know
is not always to notice.

To notice,
is not fully to know,

but is the foundation
of all knowing.

And when the noticed
is even begun
to be known,

then, in the orchard,
knowing
the noticed,
is only
partial knowing,

for noticing starts all over again,
and the knower
vanishes in understanding.

YOU'RE SUPPOSED TO NOTICE

1

The farmworker,
walking the overpass
across the freeway:

his morning shadow slinks along
the sunlit north wall.

2

The whirling swallows
descend to the water
in the roadside ditch:

catching flying insects
the rest of us can't see
is real hard work!

THE SHELL IN AUGUST

Like the shell on the window-sill,
bought how many years ago,
and now and then
held to the rose ear,

is the sorrowing wave sound
of this summer's ebb-tide;
low spread,
and long withdrawal.

CONCERNING VINES AND FIG TREES

Where the old fig tree died —
rotten at the heart, bearing fewer and still
fewer
leaves, and fruit —

see, a new small sapling,
out of his roots;
hands up, receiving glory!

The smallest of the Muscat vines:
an old gentleman,
trimmed to his bud-length:

survivor of how many Januarys?
still, seeking his nesting-bird;
still,
with some shelter in him.

FLAILING BRANCHES

In spite of the north
wind, the doves ...

one's nesting, so
the other forages
while the wind
blows her voice ...

wild quiet
in the depths
of their calls ...

AT THAT MOMENT

the light
three hours before
sundown
shows (against sky)
                              (earliest fading)
the leaves of the American
black walnut

playing
the blues!
            on
cool
delicate

(trembling but
got it
just right)

fingers

ASPIRATIONS

The moth at the window knocking:
O how beautiful to immerse my
self: in that flame:
and it's only a light bulb
at nine in the evening

The cat leaping way up
to the top of the reed organ:
now it's silent:
up here I am proud, successful
a decorative captain

VOICES

After the briefest
of spring showers,

so loud were the gone-wild
pigeons in the barn,
their calling

so turbulent of
gratitude,

(and for this: mere
puddles to drink from,
when no hawk is
overhead),

I just came short
of following
their cloudy
liquid speech.

TWO TROPICAL POEMS

1

The palm trees
keep unfolding
leaves of sacred wisdom
which only the birds at the feeder
perfectly understand

2

Rising to the surface
the many koi recognize each other
without breathing
their names

JUST ABOUT AFTER

The last slice of grapefruit
on the red plate,
the last gulp of wine
in the plastic coffee
cup.

Where are we going
now?
Where are the
nymphs? the deified
heroes? the

old Nile gods,

those
striding:

animal-
heads?

AT THE HEART OF THINGS

The tossed pebble knocks
the wall of the water tank
before starting
its long;
plunge:

.

then from the depths,

what spirit's grave
answering
call?

BOTTOM DOWN

At the bottom of the picture
puzzle these few
jointed lines of brown;
earth of a forest in Sweden?
a Pennsylvania
barn? where's the piece that will tell us?
still, in the
box it came in? — a New England
fishing-boat's dark
wave.

Now, the music of those young
long ago evenings,
the "I
found it", yet comes up from
beside the newspaper;
the other time the lost piece
was taken away from the dog.

That day the puzzle, complete,
resolved at last, went home;
while, under the rug
below the tall
chest of drawers, some clue
still lay

sleeping.

STATEMENT

for everything that
breeds, loves,

hopes, wants
to be
comforted,

lives, even lets
live, —

there waits, outside, [or
worse, in-
side]

a blind, unwitting,
terrible mouth.

THE COPS, THE RACERS

Around and around they go:
on TV — cruising freeways,
daring, on elliptical tracks.

Their speed is incessant. Circling
or pursuing, they are always right.
Thousands, watching, agree.

Nothing beautiful is made,
no one wounded is healed.

No pure golden
vision appears;
no creature, dying,
is raised from the dust.

THE GUEST

If you invite him to lunch,
he will disregard
the computer;
not knowing
what it might be for: and also,
the car outdoors.

But the pomegranate tree, the olives,
the figs:
if he comes to you,
he'll understand.

Try him with fish,
he'll enjoy, and share!
a honeycomb.
Speaks all languages.
Let him talk;
you will listen; and learn.

Wine, he will bless. Did it once,
twice. Do yours again.

He sits quietly;
then soft as a ghost,
he'll disappear;

leave you and me
to ourselves.

BEYOND

Beyond the sheltered steps, beyond the
roses bracketed
climbing over all,
the walnut trees aiming for sky,

is blue: not the hard
artists' enamel;
a Pacific blue,

see it clouding slightly, as
wind brings from the Bay
mist to haze the color, cool the temperature
down,

and the breath of the light white wind
is the last gasp of hauled-up albacore, the
final
prayers of sailors,

whose boats broached,
filled,
left them
alone,

yesterday,
years ago.

SUMMER FAN POEM

The north-north-
west wind spins the
north window
fan around & around.

It repeats as we all do,
the same thoughts:

where is the wind blowing from?
what is the use of
craft
after the false beginning?

All our lines are
converging,
yes, to what
vanishing
point?

A WALK TO THE BRIDGE

As we walked along
the bridge, from under it
soared the thousand wheeling
crying swallows,

a cloud of birds, defending their
hidden nestlings;
calling each others' names,

which are Summer,
Dance-in-Air,
and Joy.

IN THE MORNING

Every twenty seconds, a quail call:
a single note;

the combine is silent,
parked somewhere in the east end
of the wheat field.
Then the alarm call,
quail in the stubble.

The rising heat, I naked for a moment,
dressing alone.

PLOWING DOWN

Beyond the window,
there's a rolling noise,
it's only neighbor's tractor
turning over
buried years.

Down goes October,
overwhelming worn-out
troubles, breaking,

breaking old
crops, last night's
sad
dreams:

for the oblivion,
the renewal,
of all-covering
earth.

WHO REMEMBERS?

last century's love?
The old tree
just about obscures
(from this
window)
the young tree

and as
down
goes
twilight,
both turn

to brown.

SOUNDS

Not too far
from this house:
quail calls: alarm!

They used to be so abundant,
here, before crops and cattle.

Now I have to drive
all the way to the end
of Road 29,
to hear them,

see them burst into the air,
and wait for wild turkeys,
a flock of twenty, there,
clucking, fleeing my car,
hastening along the fence line.

FALL PLOWING

The dark smoke springs up
from the diesel tractor's stack

and disperses slowly
in still blue air

like your hopes
and my fears.

BACKDROP

The sun backs
the glow
of the paper-thin
clouds over
a stage set of
willows
in the neighboring
distance

All still: one in the
afternoon
is too early for
the next
storm scene in this
lately shaken
October show

In the second act
as I remember
birds fly for shelter through the rain

THE SOUND OF THE RAIN

came through
under the sound of the fridge.

Deeper first,
that low beginning:
then open, lighter,
as the fridge finally shut off.

Rain
— turned around;
lay down;
played;
settled in:

and then began its old
story:

it tells itself
how it washed away mountains,
made rivers to flood,
exposed ancient bones.

AT SUNRISE

1

A cool breeze,
right on the forehead;
me:
safe under one
blanket or two.

The diesel starts
once, twice, three-four times,
catches!
at last:

starts plowing up
neighbor's
acres.

2

At sundown,
the dry gold wild-oats
under the sea-wind,
blackbirds hunting
their seeds, smallest of all.

.

THE LITTLE SNOWMAN

in his plastic globe
has only soap chips
to fall around him.

He's never seen
real snow, hasn't heard about it
nor heard the carols;

all that liquid
in his ears.

All he might feel, know:
right side up and
upside down.

Pray for him:
may he always be loved,
brought out at Christmas,
may his humble planet
never break,

let nothing sorrowful
to him befall,
any of the fatal accidents
of the pure and small.

LITTLE CHRISTMAS EVE IN COLORADO

The tree robed
in winter light.

The dove-gray
of heavy cloud.

The dark of clear water emerging
from the canyon snow bank.

The depth of untraveled snow.

One blue jay, flying low.

The hearth fire of memory
everyone gazes into.

The snap of a pine log,
in the breathing
peace.

DAY AFTER CHRISTMAS IN THE MOUNTAINS

A wraith stalks down the mountainside:
the first twist
of blowing snow.

TWO OWL POEMS

1

The bird outside,
it's the end of winter,

invades
March dark.

As in fluting spring,
evening
shuts up
other calls,

blackbirds,
larks, doves:
you name them,

his, the only
deep voice,
is a soft
clarinet.

2

Low notes and lower:

two owls before dawn
mourning at the wake
of old darkness.

ZOO POEM

Carnivores have eyes in front:
They hafta
hunt.

Herbivores have eyes on-side:
They needta

(hide).

UNDER SEA WIND

Now, see, how
the big nearer tree
waves more slowly
(except the trailing
branches)
than the little walnut's
wholeness;

three, springs, old,
and it hasn't leapt up yet
flourishing its green dangly catkins:

now, who will lie down today;
anywhere, for sleep, for love; and who
will not get up?

How many years
will both trees
wave back to me?

WHERE POEMS COME FROM

(you asked, didn't you?)

Well now,
there's this highway on the
east side of the Rockies
or maybe it's the Sierra Nevada:
it's the Interstate, you go
down it or maybe it's north,
depends on which way you're
coming from and then you turn left, or
depending it's
right and you climb out of the
valley with the old volcanic
cones and then gradually
it becomes hilly, and then you're in the
MOUNTAINS:

ʌʌʌʌʌ
ʌʌʌʌʌʌʌ⁄ᴂ\ ʌʌʌ
ʌ ʌ ʌʌʌʌʌ

and from your base, the
yellow-pine lodge,
a long dangerous hike
(rattlers, sudden rock falls)
to the spring:

pouring from granite,
filtered through

old lava flows.

I've been there a couple of times, it's the
finest purest spring
water
anywhere, —

(Yes, I've had to turn back often,
I can't always be sure of the trail;
maybe you'll get lost, too),
but I'll tell you one thing,

they don't sell that spring
water, in plastic
bottles, anywhere;

you must risk your life
to find it.

EL SUEÑO / THE DREAM

In a faraway
brown country

ocean crashes against
barren mountains

they play wooden flutes
profound drums

they tell their children
their proud red history

still they are a tall
quiet people

3 A. M.

1

I can silence
that unhappy fly
by turning off
the bedside light

the hungry mosquito
she was here
at twilight
is a very different
animal

2

The light in the north window
is merely a reflection
of my lamp

it is the form of all illusions
I used to think it was a house, a parked truck
realized quickly
it couldn't be a star

now that I am awake,
I can turn it on
or off

SPIDER

I scoop the astonished
thirsty spider
out of the bathroom sink

she falls to the floor
with a faint plop

nobody else hears the sound
yet it troubles, surely
the fostering earth

IN A MOMENT

The air is almost
rain. The faded gold
of old-century
paintings. Now no
sweet light
even at early
afternoon.

All of us
hold our
breath. The
first rain
drops

surely coming
soon.

THE SINGER

The owl in the oak tree
called from the parking lot
behind the apartment building
the only year I was there

it sounded like a basketball
bounced up and down bobobobo
just before a jump shot
or like the bassoon music
Mozart wrote for a friend

after I graduated
they cut down the oak tree
wrecked the wooden apartment building
where there had been love
and put up a new one
all cement

last winter the owl called
here, in the country,
somewhere, a mile off,
maybe inward, on
Road 29

now: was it the same owl,
or one other of
the same fugitive
species?

who: is that owl? well,
she's safe near me
I have little money
and no power
over soft wild songs

MAYBE DIRE, MAYBE NOT

What's this, coming down
the post-midnight road?
A pair of headlights, silent as a spectral visitant
in a gothic poem. They slide
out of sight, I return to my book.
Now there on the blanket
is a small bug, staring up at me,
twiddling its feelers
round and around. A messenger from
the Other World, are you? Just never watched
a human read before? Well, be off,
you two great inconsequential
warnings. Methinks: you were
intended for some other wight.
I'm turning the light
out, going back to sleep.

NECESSARY

There are two ways
to be humbled:

write a poem
in the face of all
those anthologies;

discover a younger,
better poet.

Or you can raise a sail
on the wide,
restless sea.

THE RETURN

We wake because we are sated with sleep —
a feast we take in with our breathing,
salted with dreams. Enough —

we emerge from sleep as from a great adventure:
like driving across the desert,
hearing a long symphony;
a thing encountered, undergone,
well spent.

Rising from sleep is as from a task accomplished,

a night over and done with:
at the last,

a date in the calendar
put away forever,
surely.

SIX IN THE MORNING

pale orange dawn light
beyond the windows
still green branches swaying
lashed by the
late summer wind

away with dreams
what are two feet for?
to arise, to stand on
to find the curious road ahead